SITING
AT
HIS
FEET

Words of Wisdom For
Women of Wisdom

By

Carmelia Bivins

A Book of Intimate Refreshing With the Lord...

Where You Can Drink From the Fountain of Life

And

Never Thirst Again

ISBN: 1-4107-3564-8 (e-book)
ISBN: 1-4107-3563-X (Paperback)

This book is printed on acid free paper.

All scripture references are taken from the New International Version of the Bible unless otherwise indicated.

1stBooks – rev. 5/14/03

DEDICATION

To my beautiful daughter,

Elizabeth Mikaela Bynoe

Who has grown into a strong, independent and wise young woman. A young woman of character who loves the Lord and who is learning how to walk gracefully with Him daily. Remember, the steps of a righteous woman are ordered by the Lord. Always seek the Lord first in all you do.

CONTENTS

INTRODUCTION

I must first give honor, glory and thanks to my Heavenly Father for placing this book into my spirit. It flows like rivers of living waters. To every woman who reads this book I greet you in the name of our Lord and Savior Jesus Christ. I speak blessings into your life in the name above every other name, the name of Jesus. I write to you these words of love, wisdom, and encouragement. These words that will set you free from every stronghold in your life if you trust in the Lord. These words that will bring you deliverance and a sense of true love, peace, joy and happiness. These words that will give you some insight, direction, and clarity as to what God has for you to do.

These words straight from the heart, because you are special, you are somebody. You are a precious jewel to behold, and you are everything that God has called you to be. You are everything that God has ordained you to be. You are who God says you are. All that God has for you, it is for you. All of the blessings and treasures that God has promised you are yours for the asking in Jesus name. Receive it, believe it and reach up and grab it in the name of Jesus.

Sitting at His Feet is a book for women. It is a book of intimate refreshing with the Lord. We as women have gone through many struggles. Many of us have endured some pain, hurt and abuse. We have many responsibilities, many duties and many hats to wear. We sometimes get to the point where we feel overwhelmed.

This book serves as a reminder that our Lord loves women too. Jesus was compassionate with women hundreds of years ago and He is still compassionate with us today. He has not forgotten or forsaken us. Whatever your struggles are take them to the feet of the Lord. Sit at His feet and release every hurt, pain, problem, concern and tear and leave it at his feet. Sit at His feet and release every heavy weight, every burden, and every care that interrupts your daily life. Sit at His feet and love Him, talk to Him, worship Him and let Him love you back. Take some "personal self time" to be intimate with the Lord.

Take off your old garment, the "old dress" because yesterday's dress is worn and torn. It's not good enough for where the Lord is taking you today. It's not good enough for today's woman. Store up all of your treasures in heaven where they will be safe. Look to God and not to man. It is God who will give you the increase on your treasures. God will cleanse you from all of your issues. You will never have to look back at them again! You are capable and equipped through the POWER of God.

From this day forward live your life on purpose, and to the fullest. You have a right to happiness. You have a right to walk in the fullness of your calling. You have a right to glorify Him and thank Him for creating you. From this day forward walk with your head held high. Remember that God will never leave you nor will He ever forsake you. He will never put more on you then you can bear.

Yours in Christ,

Minister Carmelia Bivins

P. O. Box 250

El Cajon, California 92022

e-mail: PRAYEDUP2@COX.NET

PART 1

Believing That You Are A Woman Of Excellence

Carmelia Bivins

For you created my inmost being; you knit me together in my mother's womb. I praise you because I am fearfully and wonderfully made; your works are wonderful, I know that full well. My frame was not hidden from you when I was made in the secret place. When I was woven together in the depths of the earth, your eyes saw my unformed body. All the days ordained for me were written in your book before one of them came to be.

Psalms 139:13-16

1

You Are...

You are **(I am)** a woman of excellence, a woman of quality, a

distinguished woman.

You are **(I am)** a special being of top quality, a woman who ranks

high in God's kingdom.

You are **(I am)** a woman of great integrity, that God created for a

particular purpose.

You are **(I am)** a woman that God has made entire, complete and

confident.

You are **(I am)** a woman who is one of a kind.

You are **(I am)** a woman who is unique, an original. When God

created you **(me)** He threw away the mold. So there is none other like

you (me).

You are **(I am)** a woman of strength and wisdom. A woman of character, who is sincere in all you **(I)** do.

You are **(I am)** a woman full of energy, full of motivation, full of discipline, full of vigor, full of power and authority in Jesus' name.

You are **(I am)** a virtuous woman, one that's good, one that's patient, a woman after God's own heart.

You are **(I am)** a woman that is understanding, filled with kindness, compassion and love for all. One who is not easily provoked, one whose cup runs over with every blessing from the Lord.

You are **(I am)** a woman who perseveres in all you **(I)** do. A woman who cannot be easily swayed. A woman who knows who you are **(I am)** and where you **(I)** stand. A woman who is sold out for Jesus.

You are **(I am)** a woman who is an intercessor and a prayer warrior. A woman who bears the infirmities of the weak.

You are **(I am)** a woman who is steadfast and persistent in prayer on behalf of family, friends and yourself **(myself)**. A woman who knows what it means to "stand" and when you **(I)** know you've done all you **(I)** can, still "stand".

You are **(I am)** a woman full of the Holy Spirit. A woman who loves God with all your **(my)** heart, mind, soul and body.

You are **(I am)** a woman of pride, glory and high self-esteem. You **(I)** have a servant's heart and you **(I)** delight in pleasing your **(my)** Lord and others.

You are **(I am)** a woman of talent. A woman with many abilities and high expectations for yourself **(myself)**.

You are **(I am)** a woman with "class". A woman who will not settle for just anything. A woman who is discerning, obedient and observant. A woman who is carefully selective in all you **(I)** do. One who delights yourself **(myself)** in how you **(I)** look, act, dress and speak.

You are **(I am)** a woman of ambition with many aspirations and desires that are pleasing to God and that line up with His word. A woman who constantly seek after the good things in life.

You are **(I am)** a woman with many capabilities and plenty of potential. A woman who will give your **(my)** very best in everything you **(I)** do to complete the task.

You are **(I am)** a woman of endurance, because you **(I)** know that the race is not given to the swift nor the battle to the strong, but to those who endure till the end.

You are **(I am)** a woman of faith, speaking those things that are not as though they already are. A woman who speaks blessings to her **(my)** own circumstances and to all who are around you **(me)**. A woman of virtue.

You are **(I am)** a woman who has been set apart for the Master's use. A woman already prepared to go where He sends you **(me)** and do what He tells you **(me)** to do.

You are **(I am)** a woman of forgiveness, not allowing past or present hurts, pains, struggles and disappointments to keep you **(me)** from soaring. A woman who realizes that God will renew your **(my)** strength when you **(I)** wait upon Him.

You are **(I am)** a woman who knows that old things are passed away, behold all things are become brand new.

You are **(I am)** a woman who is wise. A woman who realizes and accepts that all of your **(my)** sins have been cast into the sea of forgetfulness never to return again.

You are **(I am)** a woman who has committed yourself **(myself)** to pick up your **(my)** cross daily to follow Christ. A woman who knows that you **(I)** have a second chance and the sky is the limit.

You are **(I am)** a woman of humility. A woman who is modest, meek, submissive, mild tempered, gentle, loving and longsuffering.

You are **(I am)** a woman who has been set free by the Holy Spirit and by the renewing of your **(my)** mind. A woman who has overcome every obstacle; acknowledging that the enemy may try to block you **(me)** but he sure can't stop you **(me)**.

You are **(I am)** a woman who is an Ambassador of Christ's kingdom. A woman who is full of grace, dignity and wisdom.

You are **(I am)** a woman of God. A woman who fears and reverences the Lord. A woman who possess the "Crowning Qualities of Womanhood".

You are **(I am)** a woman who is special. A woman who is happy and joyful to be a child of the Almighty King. A woman who will mount up on wings as an eagle. A woman who will run and not be weary. A woman who will walk and not faint, as long as you **(I)** wait upon the Lord.

You are **(I am)** a woman of excellence and you **(I)** will succeed and excel. "Have a heart devoted to serving God, abide in His word and faithfully commit yourself to prayer on a daily basis". *You are…who God says you are.*

Carmelia Bivins

Rejoice in the Lord always. I will say it again: Rejoice! Let your gentleness be evident to all. The Lord is near. Do not be anxious about anything, but in everything, by prayer and petition, with thanksgiving, present your requests to God. And the peace of God, which transcends all understanding, will guard your hearts and your minds in Christ Jesus.

Philippians 4:4-7

2

A Virtuous Woman, That's You!

Proverbs 31:10 says: *Who can find a virtuous woman? For her price is far above rubies.*

Proverbs 31:11 says: *The heart of her husband does safely trust in her so that he will have no need of spoil.*

Proverbs 31:12 says: *She will do him good and not evil all the days of her life.*

A virtuous woman is a versatile woman. A virtuous woman is a woman who is every woman. A virtuous woman is not found in every woman, but she is found in those who loves and obeys the Lord. A virtuous woman is an excellent woman. A virtuous woman can always smile about the good and the bad, the highs and the lows, the ups and the downs, the fortunate and the unfortunate, the positive and the negative. A **virtuous** woman keeps on going through the aches and the pains. She realizes that many depend upon her. Although there is a long list of **virtuous** women, let's look at the characteristics and commitments of two kinds of **virtuous** women. The married virtuous woman and the single **virtuous** woman.

If you are a married **virtuous** woman you are a woman of noble character and you are tolerable of many things. You always have the welfare of your family in mind. Many times you forget about your own needs or you put them on hold to make certain that everybody else is happy. A married **virtuous** woman learns how not to criticize, murmur or complain.

You are seldom able to find the quiet quality time needed to sit at the feet of the Lord and bask in His presence. But you soon find out that you can spend your quiet quality time with the Lord early in the morning before the sun comes up or you can get it late at night before going to bed, while everyone else is already sleeping. This is your time to find peace and renew your strength for the days to come. A married **virtuous** woman is one who is upright and respectable. You have your husband's "back" at all times. You not only pray for your husband and his shortcomings, you also pray for your children, yourself and your own shortcomings. You gladly support your husband in whatever he does. You encourage him to go on and you listen to him when he needs a listening ear. A married **virtuous** woman's footsteps are ordered by the Lord.

If you are a single **virtuous** woman, you seek to be a woman after God's own heart. Your focus is on the Lord, on your children, on your community, and on your job. Your mind is constantly wondering what you can do to help others. How you can encourage someone else. You always have a smile for someone who might be struggling even though many times you are struggling yourself. You always have a hug for someone who might be feeling lonely even though you may be feeling lonely yourself. You always have a kind word to lift someone up who may be feeling down even though you may be down yourself. You seek the Lord all the days of your life. You always make it your business to seek first the kingdom of God in all you do and you take everything you plan to do to the Lord in prayer. You know that God is preparing you for what He has already purposed for your life. You know how to sit at His feet and wait in

His presence because you know how to hear His voice. You follow the Lord's instructions no matter what. A single **virtuous** woman's footsteps are ordered by the Lord. You constantly study the word of God because you find it to be a lamp unto your feet and a light unto your path. You find it to be soothing to you when you might be going through something. A single **virtuous** woman keeps her head held high because you know who you are in Christ Jesus.

Why does a married **virtuous** woman do the things that she does? Because a married **virtuous** woman knows that she and her mate have become one flesh. He is her better half and she is his better half. Two better halves make a better and complete whole. When he struggles, she struggles. When he is going through, she goes through. When he is burdened down, she is burdened down. She feels what he feels and he feels what she feels. A married **virtuous** woman stands in the gap for her husband and family.

Why does a single **virtuous** woman do the things that she does? Because she knows that none of us are perfect. We've all made mistakes in our life. Experience is the best teacher, so we learn from our past mistakes and grow from them. A single **virtuous** woman has learned to be honest, kind and soft spoken. She is quick to listen and slow to speak. She is careful what comes out of her own mouth. When a single **virtuous** woman speaks she speaks words of life. A single **virtuous** woman does not tolerate gossip or cliques. Cliques represent a "carnal corral" and a single **virtuous** woman knows how to stay away from them. A single **virtuous** woman is one who bends but never breaks under the pressures of life. She has wisdom to run into the arms of God for love, comfort, advise, support and stability, and not into the arms of the enemy.

I know many of you are trying to find all of these **virtuous** qualities within yourself. Even though you may not seem to find them or see them in yourself they are there. When God made woman, He stepped back, took a look and said, "it is good, very good", and then He broke the mold after making each one of us. We are carefully and uniquely made. We are fearfully and wonderfully made. So you see you really are unique and there is none like you. You are one of a kind.

If you cannot see or find the **virtuous** qualities in yourself right now it's okay because believe it or not, others do.

Carmelia Bivins

Let the wise listen and add to their learning...

Proverbs 1:5

3

Life Lessons

Everything that we do in this life is a process of learning. Oftentimes we have to take the good with the bad, the ups with the downs and the bitter with the sweet. We all make mistakes along the way. The key is to learn from our mistakes. We all fall down sometimes. The key is to not stay down but to get back up again. We all get talked about sometime. The key is to ignore it and stay focused. We all get left out sometime. The key is to smile any how and move forward in the Lord. He will never overlook us or leave us out. We will always be included with him. Keep on pressing toward the mark of the high calling in Christ Jesus. It's not how fast you run this race of life, but it's the fact that you endure until the end and don't give up. We are learning everyday. Through our process of daily learning we are:

Learning to Love

Learning to Talk

Learning to Appreciate

Learning to Pray

Learning to Submit

Learning to Yield

Learning to Pay Attention

Learning to Accept

Learning to Encourage

Learning to Fast

Learning to Read

Learning to Study

Learning to Meditate

Learning to Praise

Learning to worship

Learning to Fellowship

Learning to Unite

Learning to Be at Peace with one another

Learning to Agree

Learning to Walk together as one

Learning to Please God

Learning to Live Holy

Learning to Be Real

Learning to Be Honest

Learning to Evaluate

Learning to Set Goals

Learning to Plan

Learning to Respect

Learning to Discover

Learning to Grow

Learning to See

Learning to Endure

Learning to Persevere

Learning to Witness

Learning to Share

Learning to Listen

Learning how Not to Gossip

Learning to Speak the Truth

Learning to Reach Out

Learning to Embrace

Learning to Be Helpful

Learning to Laugh

Learning to Cry

Learning to Heal

Learning to Be Happy

Learning to Dream

Learning to Forgive

Learning to Move On

Learning to Trust

Learning to Increase Your Faith

Learning to Seek

Learning to Be Wise

Learning to Be Patient

Learning to Be Kind

Learning to Be Humble

Learning to Be Holy

Learning to Be Submissive

Learning to Hope

Learning to Wait Upon the Lord

Learning to Stand

Learning to Serve

Learning to Be Obedient

Learning to Create

Learning to Overcome

Learning to Follow

Learning to Lead

Learning to Put Others First

Learning to Be a Winner

Learning to Communicate

Learning to Be Understanding

Learning to Rejoice

Learning to Be Free

Learning to Prosper

Learning to Be the Best that You can Be

Learning to live life on purpose because God made you on purpose with a divine purpose in mind for every one of you. He has a divine plan in mind for every one of you.

Our job is to find out what that purpose and plan is and don't give up, trying to find it. Every step we take we are learning. Every move we make we are learning. Each lesson gets a little easier. Each step gets a little shorter. Each smile gets a little brighter. Each round goes a little higher. Don't give up now because your breakthrough is about to take place. Your miracle is on the way.

And we know that in all things God works for the good of those who love him, who have been called according to his purpose. For those who God foreknew he also predestined to be conformed to the likeness of his Son, that he might be the firstborn among many brothers. And those he predestined, he also called; those he called, he also justified; those he justified, he also glorified.

Romans 8:28-30

4

Women on the Move for Christ,

Living Life on Purpose

What does doing something on purpose mean? Purpose is doing something intentionally. It means that you are doing something with a specific goal and a specific mission in mind. Since we know that God created us on purpose, we want to live life to the fullest and on purpose. Purposely pleasing God. Purposely loving, purposely caring, purposely being all that God has ordained you to be.

Purpose is purpose-filled. All of the things listed below are purpose-filled in God's kingdom. When we do the work of the Lord it is to be purpose-filled. It is to be exciting. It is to be filling not just for yourself but also for others. We are women and we are blessed. As you receive your abundance of blessings don't hold those blessings in the palm of your hand and close your fingers around them.   Pass them on so that somebody else can be blessed too.

Purpose is blessing others. As you release your blessings by blessing

others you are making room for your new blessings.

Purpose is faith

Purpose is hope

Purpose is determination

Purpose has an aim

Purpose has a meaning

Purpose gives direction

Purpose is moving

Purpose has a plan

Purpose has a vision

Purpose is deliberate

Purpose is a desire

Purpose is useful

Purpose is an expectation

Purpose is beneficial

Purpose is being ambitious

Purpose is persistent

Purpose is profitable

Purpose is necessary

Purpose is intentional

Purpose has a mission

Purpose is profitable

Purpose is necessary

Purpose is essential

Purpose is required

Purpose is certain

Purpose is progress

Our sole purpose for being created is to serve the Lord. It is time to commit yourself to serving the Lord fully, personally, and wholly. We have been called to carry out His purpose and as we do we will find our own purpose.

And we know that in all things God works for the good of those who love him, who have been called according to his purpose. (Romans 8:28)

Carmelia Bivins

Let your conversation be always full of grace, seasoned with salt, so that you will know how to answer everyone.

Colossians 4:6

5

Women of Wisdom Speaking Words of Wisdom

Women of Wisdom speak wholesome, healing, soothing, kind, encouraging, truthful, peaceful words.

THERE IS POWER IN THE WORDS WE SPEAK! LIFE AND

DEATH ARE IN THE POWER OF THE WORDS WE SPEAK!

The tongue has the power of LIFE and DEATH and those who love it will eat its fruit. (Proverbs 18:21)

What damage can we do when we do not learn how to speak positive, godly words? We should always be slow to speak and quick to listen.

Words Can:

Curse instead of bless. Lie instead of speak the truth. Build up or tear down. Lift up or breakdown. Make or break a person. They can hinder or heal. Make you feel wanted or unwanted. Love or hate. Be beautiful or ugly. Encourage or discourage. Be strong or weak. Be forgiving or unforgiving. Be good or bad. Sick or well.

Words Can:

Make you feel respected or disrespected. Make your heart feel full or empty, heavy or light. Make you laugh or cry. They can make you bold or afraid. They can make you live in the light or keep you in the darkness. Make you feel positive or negative. Keep you in bondage or make you free. Make you live life to the fullest or make you cease to live. They can make you happy or sad, joyful or angry. They can enable you to make it or disable you from trying. They can help you to accomplish your dreams, hopes and desires or shatter every hope of ever making it. They can accuse, abuse and misuse. They can be pleasing or displeasing, pure or filthy.

BAD WORDS ARE NOT NECESSARY AND

CAN BE AVOIDED THROUGH SELF-CONTROL.

Words Can:

Be believing or unbelieving. They can create success or failure. They can sting or soothe. They can cut like a knife or be gentle as a feather. They can cause you to be faithful or faithless. They can keep you focused or blind you. They can mend or tear. They can make your day bright or gloomy.

Words Can:

Be godly or godless. They can represent the Lord or represent satan. They can be bitter or sweet. They can consecrate or desecrate (be foul). They can keep you near or take you far. They can cause

31

you to stay down or make you rise up. Be discerning or foolish. They can be a destroyer or a deliverer. They can make you do right or make you do wrong. Learn how to tame your tongue and speak blessings instead of curses and peace instead of doom.

There are those who speak rashly, like the piercing of a sword, but the tongue of the wise brings healing. (Proverbs 12:18)

"THINK BEFORE YOU SPEAK!"

Arise, and go down to the potter's house, and there I will cause thee to hear my words. Then I went down to the potter's house, and, behold, he wrought a work on the wheels. And the vessel that he made of clay was marred in the hund of the potter: so he made it again another vessel, as seemed good to the potter to make it.

Jeremiah 18:2-4 (KJV)

6

A Vessel Fit for the Master's Use

II Timothy 2:20,21 says: In a large house there are articles not only of gold and silver, but also of wood and clay; some for noble purposes and some for ignoble. If a man cleanses himself from the latter; he will be an instrument for noble purposes, made holy, useful to the Master and prepared to do any good work.

When God chose you to be His vessel He knew you lacked much of what was needed to be used as a *Vessel of Honor*. He knew you were an empty, hollow unfeeling vessel. But God being the God that He is, also knew that you could not fix yourself, you could not fill yourself and you could not change yourself. God in His omniscience recognized the work that had to take place in you in order for Him to have you where He wanted you to be. To that place of courage and character fit for the Master's Use.

When no one else loved you, it was your Heavenly Father who held you close to His bosom to let you know that He loves you. When no one else believed in you, it was your Heavenly Father who whispered in your ear to let you know that He believes in you.

When no one else seemed to care about you, it was your Heavenly Father who held you close in His strong arms to let you know that He cares for you. When no one else would listen to you, it was your Heavenly Father who gave you all of His precious attention to listen to what you had to say. When no one else had time for you, it was your Heavenly Father who gave you all of the time that you needed. When no one else would recognize the good in you, it was your Heavenly Father who made you realize and remember that He created you and when He did the results were good, very good. God doesn't waste His precious time making junk.

The love that God has for you is deeper than the water in the deepest sea. The love that God has for you is wider than the widest mountain. The love that God has for you, is more then the sand on the beach or the stars in the sky. The love that God has for you surpasses all understanding.

You are an earthen vessel that is being perfected step by step, day by day, hour by hour, minute by minute, second by second, to be like Him. The good work that God has began in you He all by Himself is able to complete it. As a vessel consecrated and committed to God you are to keep yourself available to Him at all times. As you submit to His will and His way, He will shape you, mold you and polish you until you come out as pure as gold. You may have come to God as a castaway pearl but in God's eye you are a treasure to behold.

When you come to God sincerely asking, seeking and knocking surrendering to Him that cracked, rusted out, worn vessel that has been hurt and stepped on, abused and misused then and only then will you leave the "Potter's" house, God's house brand new. Every crack will be fixed, every imperfection will be made whole, every weak spot will be made strong and every dark, dull, rusted area will be cleansed and shined.

Then you will know that old things have passed away and all things have become new. That includes you; *A Vessel Fit For the Master's Use!*

Many times we feel worn out and torn apart. We feel broke, busted and disgusted. It isn't for us to worry and it isn't for us to fret. It's for us to go down to the Potter's house and jump on the wheel and let him begin to work on us and through us. He restores and heals every broken vessel. We know that only the Lord can correct our wrongs and imperfections and make us new and whole again. Don't give up when you are going through. Don't give up when you feel like you've been broken in two. Go down to the Potter's repair shop and receive your free overhaul. Your warranty will never run out. It isn't stamped limited warranty because each time you need to visit the Potter's house He'll be there to complete the repair. With Christ there are no limits.

Carmelia Bivins

Finally, brothers (sisters), whatever is true, whatever is noble, whatever is right, whatever is pure, whatever is lovely, whatever is admirable—if anything is excellent or praiseworthy—think about such things.

Philippians 4:8

7

Keeping Lust Up Under the Blood

LUST IS LIVING UP UNDER satan's CONTROL

Lust is living up under satan's temptation.

L=Living

U=Under

S=satan's

T=Temptation

As women of God we are to live pure, holy, righteous, blameless lives. Resist satan's control and his temptations and he will flee from you. Yield not to temptation because when you do it leads to sin. Sin eventually leads to death. READ, STUDY and PRAY!

Here are some scriptures that will help you to walk in the spirit so that you will not fulfill (act upon) the lust of the flesh.

Watch and pray so that you will not fall into temptation. The spirit is willing but the body is weak. (Matthew 26:41)

Put to death, therefore, whatever belongs to your earthly nature: sexual immorality, impurity, lust, evil desires, and greed, which is idolatry. (Colossians 3:5)

Therefore, I urge you, brothers (sisters), in view of God's mercy, to offer your bodies as living sacrifices, holy and pleasing to God—this is your spiritual act of worship. (Romans 12:1)

Submit yourselves, then, to God. Resist the devil, and he will flee from you. Come near to God and he will come near to you. (James 4:7,8)

So I say, live by the Spirit, and you will not gratify the desires of the sinful nature. For the sinful nature desires what is contrary to the

Spirit, and the Spirit what is contrary to the sinful nature. They are in conflict with each other, so that you do not do what you want. But if you are led by the Spirit, you are not under law. (Galatians 5:16-18)

Do not love the world or anything in the world. If anyone loves the world, the love of the Father is not in him (her). For everything in the world—the cravings of sinful man (woman), the lust of his (her) eyes and the boasting of what he (she) has and does—comes not from the Father but from the world. The world and its desires pass away, but the man (woman) who does the will of God lives forever.
(I John 2:15-17)

For the grace of God that brings salvation has appeared to all men (women). It teaches us to say No to ungodliness and worldly passions, and to live self-controlled, upright and godly lives in this present age, while we wait for the blessed hope—the glorious appearing of our Great Lord and Savior, Jesus Christ, who gave himself for us to redeem us from all wickedness and to purify for

himself a people that are his very own, eager to do what is good.
(Titus 2:11-14)

When you seek after the things of God you will stay on the right road. It is when you begin to cross the road and think you can get away with experimenting in what some like to call "small" sin that you lose your balance. Sin is sin, no matter how big or small. Keep your flesh up under the blood and you will not gratify the desires of your sinful nature (flesh). Make your flesh submit to you don't submit to it. You are to have control over your fleshly nature and your fleshly desires. Do it by saturating yourself in God's word. His word will keep you cleansed from the inside out and from the outside in. If you allow the lust of sin to get into your spirit it will choke the word of God and smother it until the word of God will no longer seem to have its proper place in your heart. When you fail to give place to the things of God then other things will take its place.

And the cares of this world, and the deceitfulness of riches, and the lusts of other things entering in, choke the word, and it becometh unfruitful. (Mark 4:19) KJV

Dearly beloved, I beseech you as strangers and pilgrims, abstain from fleshly lusts which war against the soul; (I Peter 2:11) KJV

Lust not only means sexual sins but it means anything that your flesh indulges in. Food, drugs, alcohol, sports, money, ect. Lust is anything that keeps you from fulfilling your God given purpose. Anything that comes between you and your walk with Christ.

Remember to walk in the Spirit and you will not satisfy the lusts of the flesh, when it rises up. Instead you will know how to turn away from temptation keeping yourself pure for the Master's use.

Do two walk together unless they have agreed to do so?

Amos 3:3

8

Keeping Your Marriage Covenant

For this reason a man will leave his father and mother and be united to his wife. And the two shall become one flesh. So they are no longer two, but one. Therefore, what God has *joined together, let not man separate. (Mark 10:7-9*

A marriage is a covenant. It is a binding agreement made by two people who are "head over heels" in love with each other. An agreement between two people who are celebrating their love for each other. An agreement between two people who know that they cannot live without the other. An agreement between two people who are prepared to stay together through sickness and health, through the ups and the downs, through the trials and tribulations, through the bitter and the sweet, through the good and the bad, for richer and for poorer until death do them part. The *"Marriage Covenant"* is an agreement that says as long as we pray together, we know that we will stay together.

In *Genesis Chapter 9*, God made a covenant that He would never again flood the earth and with that covenant He sends His *"Rainbow of Love"* to remind us of His agreement with us that will never be broken. Have you ever noticed that quite often God's *"Rainbow of Love"* appears after a storm and a cool shower of rain? He's reminding us that even though we go through many, many tests and trials, even though we go through distress and frustration, and with all that we endure, His covenant, His *"Rainbow of Love"* still stands and it will never ever fade away. He will never break it.

The *"Marriage Covenant"* is like God's *"Rainbow of Love"*. If every color of the rainbow had a meaning behind it, it would symbolize and represent a marriage and help us to understand and remember the *"Marriage Covenant"* between husband and wife.

Yellow would be the love and the laughter, the life and the light in a marriage. *Orange* would be the happiness and the cheerfulness, the health, strength and sweetness in a marriage. *Green* would be the growth and the freshness, the obedience and the tolerance in a marriage. ***Blue*** would be the storm and the frustration, the differences and the unexpected in a marriage. ***Purple*** would be the purpose and the will to push forward together in a marriage. It would be the communication, agreeing, listening and understanding in a marriage. ***Pink*** would be the embarrassing moments, learning to submit, to respect each other and the patience that is needed in a marriage.

The *"Rainbow of Love"* has many colors as in a marriage. It all comes along with loving and learning all about another person. It comes along with growing and maturing together and remembering not to give up because it is an ongoing process that will become stronger as the days turn into weeks and the weeks turn into months and the months turn into years. Perfect love will cast out all fear. Even though the good and the bad, the ups and the downs, and the sickness and the health will come and go, the *"Rainbow of Love"*, the *"Marriage Covenant"* will still remain and it will out last all else.

The husband and the wife will always remember that the *"Rainbow of Love"* will get them through anything. No matter what it is, true love will never die and it will never be forgotten. Isn't that just like God to give us the greatest reminder of all, on how "not" to break a covenant?

Always keep your marriage before the Lord in prayer. Prayer should be the foundation of everything that we do. Prayer is the glue that hold things together that might otherwise fall apart. When you pray, it moves the heart of God and He will move on your behalf when you sincerely ask Him in prayer.

PART 2

Poetry

Carmelia Bivins

I lift up my eyes to the hills—where does my help come from? My help comes from the Lord, the Maker of heaven and earth. He will not let your foot slip—he who watches over you will not slumber; indeed, he who watches over Israel will neither slumber nor sleep. The Lord watches over you—the Lord is your shade at your right hand; the sun will not harm you by day, nor the moon by night. The Lord will keep you from all harm—he will watch over your life; the Lord will watch over your coming and going both now and forevermore.

Psalm 121

9

God Never Sleeps Nor Slumbers

Isn't it great to know a God who never sleeps nor slumbers?

With Him you will always be above and never ever under.

He sits way high and looks way low on everyone of you,

He began a good and perfect work in you and in you He is not

through.

He knows every little move you make and every single breath you

take, He knows your every thought,

To follow God to lean on Him is something that must be learned and

taught.

He is a gentle God, a precious God. He cares for all His children one

by one,

You know He loves you unconditionally because He sent Jesus Christ

His one and only Son.

He knows you personally it is He who formed you in your mother's

womb,

He already knows your destiny and He'll be there when you start to

bloom.

When you look straight ahead don't be swayed seek Him for all you

do,

Not only will He shower you with blessings but your mother, father,

brother and your sister too.

He has a divine purpose and plan for everyone who confesses "all"

their sin,

Just live by what the Bible says and you will surely win.

One thing I know that you must do is love Him with all your heart and

soul and mind,

You must also love your neighbor as yourself and then be extra kind.

Isn't it great to know a God who never sleeps nor slumbers?

He watches every move you make He's with you every step you take,

Let him order your footsteps, give you direction, wisdom, instruction

and a shield of protection.

He knows your going outs and He knows your coming ins,

It is Him who has made a way for you to be forgiven for your sins.

You can call Him "Daddy" late in the midnight hour,

He hears you when you call on His great and mighty power.

He won't turn His back on you for He's a God of a second chance,

He'll be right there with His arms open wide His love He will

enhance.

For you His grace is sufficient He blesses you each day,

God is an excellent and mighty God He'll work out every problem

just as long as you obey.

Isn't it great to know a God who never sleeps nor slumbers?

Now the Lord is the Spirit, and where the Spirit of the Lord is, there is freedom.

2 Corinthians 3:17

10

Where the Spirit of the Lord Is

Where the spirit of the Lord is it brings about a sense of

interdependence and total liberty,

Where the Spirit of the Lord is it brings a welcome peace of mind and

much needed relief,

Where the Spirit of the Lord is we can declare victory,

Where the Spirit of the Lord is there is no doubt, no strife, no

unbelief.

Where the Spirit of the Lord is there is no more being put down and

rejected as victim,

Where the Spirit of the Lord is there will always be everlasting

freedom,

Where the Spirit of the Lord is you are forgiven for guilt, shame and

conviction,

Where the Spirit of the Lord is you will find a declaration of affection and protection.

Where the Spirit of the Lord is there is achievement, understanding, development and growth,

Where the Spirit of the Lord is there is insight and knowledge all of both,

Where the Spirit of the Lord is there is no fear because it has been replaced with peace, love, joy and happiness,

Where the Spirit of the Lord is you are chosen by God a holy vessel that is anointed, equipped and blessed.

Where the Spirit of the Lord is you will rise above every lie told and every trick and every attack that the enemy tried to impose.

Where the Spirit of the Lord is if you are chained by bondage they will fall off and you will be set free,

Where the Spirit of the Lord is He will restore unlimited strength and your life will once again become completely whole,

Where the Spirit of the Lord is there will be unlimited rest for your weary soul,

Where the Spirit of the Lord is you know who you are, you know

where you stand,

you've stood the trials and tribulations, you've passed the test and

now it's in God's hand,

Where the Spirit of the Lord is you will be refreshed and renewed.

You will labor in

God's vineyard and do your absolute best,

Where the Spirit of the Lord is your cup will overflow with goodness

and mercy and run over the brim,

Where the Spirit of the Lord is you are guaranteed to gain all spiritual

wisdom and sound judgement, and you will be destined to win.

Because the Spirit of the Lord lives within you He will be with you

everywhere you go,

He will live and dwell inside of you this you must surely know,

Don't grieve the Spirit of the Lord go where He tells you to go,

He will be your Comforter and your Guide for the Bible tells us so.

"Where the Spirit of the Lord is there is Liberty"

Enter his gates with thanksgiving and his courts with praise;
give thanks to him and praise his name.

Psalms 100:4

11

Thank You Lord

Thank you Lord for loving me,

Thank you Lord for setting me free,

Thank you Lord for lifting me up,

Thank you Lord for filling my cup,

Thank you Lord for me you have blessed,

Thank you Lord for me you caressed

Thank you Lord for making me well,

Thank you Lord for delivering me from the grips of hell,

Thank you Lord for a strong sound mind,

Thank you Lord except in you there is no greater joy that I can find,

Thank you Lord for all of the tests,

Thank you Lord for giving me sweet rest,

Thank you Lord for your awesome power,

Thank you Lord for being my Strong Tower,

Thank you Lord for glory divine,

Thank you Lord for teaching me to be kind,

Thank you Lord for giving me peace,

Thank you Lord for a total release,

Thank you Lord for your word gives me life,

Thank you Lord for it takes away strife,

Thank you Lord for wiping away every tear,

Thank you Lord for taking away every fear,

Thank you Lord for Intercessory Prayer,

Thank you Lord for You are always there,

Thank you Lord for being near and not far,

Thank you Lord for you are my shining star,

Thank you Lord for the righteous road,

Thank you Lord for lifting my load,

Thank you Lord for forgiving my sins,

Thank you Lord for in You I win,

Thank you Lord for the battle is won,

Thank you Lord for the greatest gift of all Jesus Christ

your one and only Son.

He who dwells in the shelter of the Most High will rest in the shadow of the Almighty. I will say of the Lord, he is my refuge and my fortress, my God in whom I trust.

Psalms 91:1,2

12

When I Look Up

When I look up I am reminded that God sits way up high and looks

way down low and He's watching over me,

When I look up I am reminded that heaven is far greater than you or I

could ever imagine it to be,

When I look up I am reminded how blessed I really am,

When I look up I long to see the face of the Great

"I Am" that "I Am",

When I look up it seems that all of my hopes and dreams come true,

When I look up I am reminded that we are not worthy but God still

loves me and you,

When I look up I am reminded that I don't have anything to fear,

When I look up I am reminded that my time is drawing near,

When I look up I wear a great bright smile rather than an awful frown,

When I look up I am reminded that one day I will wear a beautiful

golden jewel filled crown,

When I look up I am reminded that God gave His one and only Son,

When I look up I am reminded that Jesus willingly hung on a tree and

died not just for me but for everyone,

When I look up it seems as though I can see God's bright

and shining face,

When I look up I am reminded that soon one day I will no longer have

to run this race,

When I look up I am reminded that the race is not given to those who

run it swiftly nor is the battle given to those who are strong,

When I look up I am reminded to be sincerely sorry, repent and ask

forgiveness for all of my wrong,

When I look up I am reminded that in Jesus I am fulfilled

and I am complete,

When I look up I am reminded that one day not long from now I will

sit at my Dear Savior's feet,

Carmelia Bivins

When I look up I am reminded just how wonderful it would be when

my "Daddy" says,

"Well done my good, obedient and faithful servant". "It is time for

you to come home to be with me,

Even now, declares the Lord, return to me with all your heart,
with fasting and weeping and mourning.

Joel 2:12

13

A Prophetic Message

Little Children It Is Time To Come Home

And now, little children, abide in him; that when he shall appear, we may have confidence, and not be ashamed before him at his coming. (I John 2:28)

When I received this message from the Lord I did not realize at that time that I was receiving a prophetic message. I don't claim to be a prophet or prophetess but I realize that God will use whom He will to get a message through. This message came from the Lord and as I was writing it I began to weep from this overwhelmingly powerful message.

I received the title, *Little Children it is Time To Come Home* because we are living in the end times and we have many Christians who have turned away from the way of Christ. The Bible tells us that in the last days many will turn away from the faith and many have turned away from the faith. This is not directed to children in as far as age is concerned, but it is directed to every child of God who know that you have stumbled and turned your ear away from the truth. It is directed to every child of God who know that you have grown stagnant, lukewarm and unconcerned about the things of God. It is directed to every child of God who know that you have turned your back on your first love. The message from the Lord is, "Return to me before it's too late. Return to me before the door is shut, and before the light goes out. Return to me while it is still day". The Lord is giving you the opportunity to repent and return to Him.

As you read the words of this powerful message allow it to saturate your spirit, your mind, and your heart. Open yourself up to what this message is saying and receive what the Lord has for you, through this message. God doesn't make any mistakes and He is not a man that He needs to lie about anything. He is a compassionate God and He will always send a message and a warning before destruction. I appeal to you to please, take this message to heart.

Carmelia Bivins

Little children it is time to come, you've strayed long enough,

Little children it is time to come home, you've been lost long enough,

Little children it is time to come home, you've been hurt long enough,

Little children it is time to come home, you've been lied on and

cheated long enough,

Little children it is time to come home, you've stayed away

long enough,

Little children it is time to come home, you've tried it on your own

long enough,

Little children it is time to come home, you've been tricked

long enough,

Little children it is time to come home, you've been devoured by the

enemy long enough,

Little children it is time to come, you've been oppressed and

depressed long enough,

Little children it is time to come home, you've been poverty stricken

and destitute long enough,

Little children it is time to come home, you've been wandering in the

wilderness long enough,

Little children it is time to come home, You've been detached from

me long enough,

Little children it is time to come home, you've been hungering and

thirsting long enough,

Little children it is time to come, you've been in rebellion

long enough,

Little children it is time to come home, you've had an attitude

long enough,

Little children it is time to come home, you've been distracted

long enough,

Little children it is time to come home, you've been blinded

long enough,

Little children it is time to come home, you've been in the darkness

long enough,

Little children it is time to come home, you've been alienated from

me long enough,

Little children it is time to come home, you've abandoned me

long enough,

Little children it is time to come home, you've missed your blessings

long enough,

Little children it is time to come home, you've stumbled long enough,

Little children it is time to come home, you've been running in the

wrong direction long enough,

Little children it is time to come home, you've turned your back on

me long enough,

Little children it is time to come home, you've been the devil's foot

stool long enough,

Little children it is time to come home, you've been sleeping with the

enemy long enough,

Little children it is time to come home, you've entertained false gods

long enough,

Little children it is time to come home, you've been tormented in your

mind long enough,

Little children it is time to come home, you've turned away from my

teaching long enough,

Little children it is time to come home, you've been battered and

abused long enough,

Little children it is time to come home, you've been broken hearted

long enough,

Little children it is time to come home, you've been sick in your mind

& body long enough,

Little children it is time to come home, you've been corrupted

long enough,

Little children it is time to come home, you've put on a façade

long enough,

Little children it is time to come home, you've lived on flattery and

vainglory long enough,

Little children it is time to come home, you've been full of pride

long enough,

Little children it is time to come home, you've played games

long enough,

Little children it is time to come home, you've fooled yourself

long enough,

Little children it is time to come home, you've been hard pressed on

every side long enough,

Little children it is time to come home, you've suffered and struggled

long enough,

Little children it is time to come home, you've been crushed

long enough,

Little children it is time to come home, you've been perplexed and

confused long enough,

Little children it is time to come home, you've been in despair

long enough,

Little children it is time to come home, you've been persecuted

long enough,

Little children it is time to come home, you've pretended like I don't

exist long enough,

Little children it is time for you to come home. I have been patient

with you. I have been

long suffering with you. I have given you time to repent,

and come home.

Little children it is time for you to return to your first love and do

your first works over.

You've been in the wilderness for too long.

The door is open for you and the candle is lit, but when the light goes

out, you will know that time is no more.

Our God is a loving, fair, gracious, kind, longsuffering God. He

doesn't allow calamity

to come upon any one of His children without sending us a warning.

He sends us fair

instruction by telling us what we need to do step by step. It's up to

every individual person to make the right choice on what you will do

with the instruction that you receive.

It is not our Father's desire that any should perish but that we all

should repent and come unto Him.

Repent then, and turn unto God, so that your sins may be wiped out,

that times of refreshing may come from the Lord, and that he may

send the Christ, who has been appointed for you—even Jesus.

(Acts 3:19,20)

Carmelia Bivins

PART 3

Keys to Fervent Effectual Prayer

Carmelia Bivins

If my people, who are called by my name, will humble themselves and pray and seek my face and turn from their wicked ways, then will I hear from heaven and will forgive their sin and will heal their land. Now my eyes will be open and my ears attentive to the prayers offered in this place.

II Chronicles 7:14,15

14

Regular Fervent Prayer, A Sure Remedy

The awesomeness of regular fervent prayer is a sure remedy for any situation. As children of God we are commanded to pray and we should have a healthy prayer life. Prayer is our open line of communication to our Heavenly Father. An open line means that we don't have to worry about a busy signal or a voice message. It means that we can go directly to the Father by simply opening up our mouths and speaking to Him what we want Him to hear. *"PRAYER IS THE KEY TO THE KINGDOM,"* our *FAITH* to believe, that whatsoever we ask in the name above any other name, the name of Jesus, shall be done, is what unlocks the door to the heavens.

Regular prayer should not only be a natural thing for us it should also be a regular habit. Habit forming prayer means that we are in constant prayer. Even when our mouths aren't moving our spirits are always praying and meditating on the Lord. We eat like clockwork, right? We should also pray like clockwork. There should be little or no deviation from our regular daily prayer lifestyle. Being intimate with God and spending quality time with Him through prayer moves His heart and makes Him happy. God is pleased with us when we talk to Him morning, noon and night. God is pleased when we sit at His feet or kneel in His presence in prayer and tell Him how much we love and adore Him for who He is and for all that He has already done.

Our worship to the Lord is another form of prayer. God is worthy of receiving our sincere worship because He is the worthy one to be worshipped and the worthy one to be adored. When we worship God we are pressing further into the spiritual realm. We are pressing to another level in our prayer. It is there that we can make sweet love to God and let Him make sweet love to us.

In worship to the Lord we are showing Him how much we love Him. We are letting Him know how much we honor Him, reverence Him and respect Him. We worship Him in the beauty of His holiness. We worship Him in the splendor of His holiness. We're giving Him the glory due His name. *(see I Chronicles 16:29).* Those who worship Him must do so in spirit and in truth. *(see John 4:24).* Worship is a personal thing. It's our opportunity to let God know how much we need Him. How much we applaud Him and reverence Him for His wonderful acts.

Fervent prayer is enthusiastic prayer. It is praying with boldness. That boldness of believing that God will answer when we come into His presence with the right attitude in prayer.

Hebrews 4:16 KJV says: Let us therefore come boldly unto the throne of grace, that we may obtain mercy, and find grace to help in time of need.

Coming boldly doesn't mean that you come with a demanding attitude trying to make God do something for you. It simply means that we have the confidence of knowing that we can approach a mighty, awesome and holy God to make our requests known unto Him.

James 5:16b KJV says: The effectual fervent prayer of a righteous man (woman) availeth much.

Our effectual fervent prayers come from being in right standing with God. When we are in right standing with the Lord we will see a remarkable change in our life as we pray effective and meaningfully to God. Our prayers will avail over anything else because they are valid with God. When we pray effectually and fervently we won't have to wonder if our prayers are getting through to God we will know that they have reached Him and that He is pleased.

When you pray, pray God's word. God honors His word and it will not return to Him void. When you pray His word it will not return to Him useless or meaningless. He will fulfill His purpose and His plan through the **"GREAT"** moving power of prayer.

Learn how to pray in all places, at all times, under every circumstance. You may not always feel like praying but prayer isn't a feeling it's an attitude. The right attitude of pressing your way through in the spiritual realm until you know that something has been broken. Pray until you sense a feeling of release. Pray until you know that something has been birthed.

I will therefore that men (women) pray every where, lifting up holy hands, without wrath or doubting. (I Timothy 2:8) KJV

It is a great joy and a wonderful experience to be able to talk to God, at anytime, in any place, under any condition and to know that He will hear you when you pray. Be humble when you pray. Decrease so that God can increase Himself even during your prayer.

If my people, who are called by my name, will humble themselves and pray and seek my face and turn from their wicked ways, then will I hear from heaven and will forgive their sin and will heal their land. (II Chronicles 7:14)

Look at what will take place when you humble yourself in prayer and seek His face. Then He will hear from heaven and will forgive our sins and will heal our land. It is an awesome privilege to talk to

God through prayer and then sit back, relax and watch Him move

mightily.   Prayer spells **Relief, Release, Deliverance** and **Freedom.**

So pray everyday and **Push**…until something happens.

Do not be anxious about anything, but in everything, by prayer and petition, with thanksgiving, present your requests to God.   And the peace of God, which transcends all understanding, will guard your hearts and your minds in Christ Jesus.

Philippians 4:6,7

15

Grasping the Art of Prayer

As we grasp the *"ART OF EFFECTUALLY PRAYING"* then we will become effective prayer warriors for Christ and mighty soldiers in His army.

Prayer is our foundation to success in Christ.

Prayer is our foundation to successful living.

Prayer will help us to know Christ more intimately and

to carry out His work.

Prayer is a Faith builder.

Prayer keeps us up when we are down.

Prayer puts purpose and meaning in our lives.

Prayer releases the stresses and pressures of life.

Prayer tears down the strongholds in our lives and in the lives of

others.

Prayer cancels out the plans of the devil.

Prayer brings love, joy, peace and happiness.

Prayer keeps us focused on the things of God.

Prayer keeps us on the straight and narrow path that

leads to eternal life.

Prayer strengthens us when we grow weak.

Prayer releases our mind, heart and spirit to do the will of God.

Prayer helps us to humble ourselves, resist the devil and

with prayer he will flee.

Prayer helps us to "just say no" to sin and to "just say yes"

to right living.

Prayer is our most effective weapon against spiritual warfare.

Prayer is our fellowship and communication with our Heavenly

Father.

Prayer changes things.

Prayer moves the heart of God and pleases Him.

Prayer helps you to live a purpose filled life.

Prayer allows you to stand in the gap for somebody else.

Prayer lets us bear the infirmities of the weak.

Prayer lets us pray for the sick and watch them recover.

Prayer lets us pray for those who are oppressed, obssessed and

depressed and watch them be delivered and set free.

Prayer is a medicine for all situations.

Ministries are birthed through prayer.

All things are possible when you pray.

There is wonder working power in prayer.

There is healing power in prayer.

There is a mighty deliverance waiting for you through

the power of prayer.

Your blessings are in your prayers.

Grasping the art of prayer makes you a true pray-er.

...men ought always to pray, and not to faint.

Luke 18:1(b) KJV

16

Be A Pray-er

Be a Pray-er everyday, because praying is a lifetime task.

Prayer

+

Faith

+

Praise

+

Worship

+

Commitment

+

Patience

+

Dedication

+

Forgiveness

+

Intercession

+

Reading

+

Studying

+

Perseverance

+

Focus=

_____

VICTORY IN JESUS

...If God is for us, who can be against us? No, in all these things we are more than conquerors through him who loved us. For I am convinced that neither death nor life, neither angels nor demons, neither the present nor the future, nor any powers, neither height nor depth, nor anything else in all creation, will be able to separate us from the love of God that is in Christ Jesus our Lord.

Romans 8:31,37,38,39

17

Prayer and Spiritual Warfare

Do we have power and authority over the devil? *Luke 10:19 says: Behold, I have given you authority to tread on serpents and scorpions, and over all the power of the enemy, and nothing will injure you. (NASB)* How can we be certain? *I John 4:4 says: You are from God, little children, and have overcome them; because greater is He who is in you than he who is in the world. (NASB)*

There are many Christians today who are "going through". They are under "spiritual attack" and in a "spiritual war" in various areas of their life simply because they do not realize that they have power and authority over the enemy and his demons. They do not realize their potential as Christians. They do not realize that they no longer have to settle for, put up with or tolerate the devil's attacks. They no longer have to live a life of fear and defeat.

On the other hand, many Christians do realize the power and authority that they have over the enemy but they are too afraid to face satan and let him know that they will no longer settle for him and his demons to destroy their life and the life of their loved ones. They refuse to exercise their power over the enemy.

There was a time we felt weak and powerless but now we are strong and powerful. There was a time that we felt like we were always beneath but now we can know that we are above. There was a time that we felt like we were the tail but now we can know that we are the head. There was a time that we felt like we were always last but now we can know that we are first. There was a time that we felt like we were always the borrowers but now we can know that we are the lenders. There was a time that we always felt poor but now we can know that we are rich in Christ Jesus. Because we do have the power and authority over the devil.

Some of us try to rationalize why we won't confront the devil by saying, If I leave him alone he will leave me alone". (NOT SO)! As long as you are on the Lord's side the devil will continuously "try" to cause problems for you. The day you made up your mind to live for Christ the devil already had you marked to take you out. He did not leave Adam and Eve alone in the garden and he will not leave us alone. He tried to tempt Jesus numerous times and he will always try to tempt us too. His major concern and his biggest concern is to steal, kill and destroy as many of us as he can. Another concern and goal that the enemy has is to try to get as many of us to fall off of our "spiritual band wagon".

Satan is a "strategist". He is highly skilled and very clever in what he does. He's sneaky and he will try to catch you off guard. The best way to avoid being caught off guard is to always be on guard. One of the biggest "boo" tactics that he has is to play mind games with us.

Many people are destroyed because they fall into the trap of letting the devil play with their mind instead of rebuking him and keeping themselves covered under the blood of Jesus Christ through the word and prayer. Satan loves to instill fear and intimidation upon us, if we let him. It all begins in your mind and in your thoughts. He knows that our mind is a powerful thing. And he also knows that whatever we think in our heart, if we think on it long enough we will become. Rebuke and refuse those mental attacks on your mind. If you are constantly having negative thoughts and an attitude of failure you can believe that it's from the enemy. Bind up those ungodly fleshly thoughts and loose thoughts of purity and lovely things. Bind up every imagination that tries to exalt itself against the knowledge of God and what He is trying to do in you and through you.

The devil knows the word of God backwards and forwards and he will use it against us any opportunity that he gets. But we as Christians must use the word of God against the enemy. Remembering that the weapons of your warfare are not carnal but mighty through God to the pulling down of strongholds. Just in case you didn't know it we have something that the devil doesn't like and it's our weapon against him. It's his enemy. His enemy is our wisdom and our knowledge of the word of God. It is imperative that we become wise in the word. The more we know about our enemy and what our options are the better off we are.

We are not fighting what is without what we can see. We are fighting what is within what we cannot see. It's a spiritual fight therefore we have to wage war in the spiritual realm.

Wisdom and knowledge is the key. The Negro College Fund for many years used a line that said, "A mind is a terrible thing to waste". Don't waste your mind or your time or your talent doing things that are contrary to the word of God. Instead saturate yourself in the word of God. There are answers to everything in Gods word. Without wisdom and knowledge we are empty, we become exhausted, we are lost and we are unprotected against the attacks of the devil.

.....*   ......*

Wisdom	With	With	With	With	Without
Is	It	It	It	It	It
Satan's	Stop	Stay	Stay	Stay	Stay
Enemy	Evil	Encouraged	Enlightened	Equipped	Empty

If you noticed every first letter of each word reading downward spells out wise. Being wise in the word is very important. It will help you to grow and mature spiritually. It all amounts up to being wise and having wisdom in all you do.

"In the end we **WIN** = <u>W</u>isdom <u>I</u>s <u>N</u>eeded. Without it, we don't have a clue."

Carmelia Bivins

Be joyful always; pray continually; give thanks in all circumstances,
for this is God's will for you in Christ Jesus.

I Thessalonians 5:16-18

18

The ABC's of Prevailing Prayer

Prayer is <u>alive!</u> It is <u>awesome</u> <u>agreement</u> in the Spirit with the Father.

Prayer is carrying the <u>burdens</u> of the weak.

Prayer is <u>communicating</u> openly and secretly with God.

Prayer teaches us the <u>dynamics</u> of being <u>dedicated</u>.

Prayer is <u>everything</u> we need. It is <u>effective</u> and <u>exciting</u>.

Prayer builds our most holy <u>Faith</u>. It is <u>filling</u> to us

when we are empty.

Prayer is <u>glorious</u>. It is <u>generous</u> <u>goodness</u> towards others.

(Interceding).

Prayer brings <u>happiness</u> and <u>harmony</u> to our life. It <u>heals</u> and it also

feeds our <u>hunger</u> for Christ.

It gives us a continuous thirst to run after Him.

Prayer is <u>intimate</u> fellowship with God. It greatly <u>impacts</u> our

Christian life.

Prayer is a <u>joyful</u> <u>journey</u> to the throne of God.

Pray is the <u>key</u> to the <u>kingdom</u>. It helps us to love and be <u>kind</u> to all.

Prayer gives <u>life</u>. It is just like <u>living</u> water.

Prayer is <u>mighty</u>, <u>magnificent</u> and <u>meaningful</u>.

Prayer is a daily <u>necessity</u>. It minister's to our <u>needs</u> morning,

noon and night.

Prayer brings us into <u>oneness</u> of mind with each other and keeps us on

<u>one</u> accord with the Father.

Prayer is <u>powerful</u> and <u>pleasing</u> to our Heavenly Father,

Prayer does not always mean <u>quantity</u> but always <u>quality</u>. It is not

how long you pray. God

will hear you when you pray sincerely.

Prayer is <u>receiving</u> from God, being <u>real</u> with God, being <u>radical</u> for

Christ and <u>reaching</u> out to Him. Prayer <u>restores</u> us, <u>renews</u> us,

<u>replenishes</u> us and <u>rejuvenates</u> us.

Prayer is <u>savoring</u> the Lord's blessings, drawing renewed <u>strength</u>

from Him and <u>seeking</u> His answers.

Prayer is simply <u>talking</u> to the Father, <u>tasting</u> of His goodness, <u>totally</u> <u>thirsting</u> after Him and <u>taking</u> back from the devil what is rightfully yours.

Prayer is <u>unforgettable</u> and <u>unselfish.</u>

Prayer is a <u>valuable</u> tool in our Christian walk.

It gives us <u>victory</u> in Jesus name.

Prayer is <u>waging</u> <u>war</u> against the devil.

Prayer is <u>x-hilerating</u> (exhilerating).

Prayer is <u>yielding</u> to the King of kings, saying <u>yes</u> to Jesus and <u>yearning</u> for more of Him.

Prayer is <u>zeal</u> and enthusiasm for Almighty God.

"Now you know your *ABC's of Prevailing Prayer*"

Carmelia Bivins

PART 4

Sitting At His Feet

Carmelia Bivins

Jesus replied: Love the Lord your God with all your heart and with all your soul and with all your mind. This is the first and greatest commandment.

Matthew 22:37,38

19

Sitting At His Feet

Dear Heavenly Father,

The Creator of the heavens and the earth. The Creator of all good and perfect things. The Rock of my salvation. My Rock in a weary land. My shelter in the time of storm. My Bridge over troubled waters. My Lily in the valley. My Bright and Morning Star. My Strongtower and my Fortress. My Redeemer and my Deliverer. My Provider and my Way out of no way. My Healer and my Problem Solver. My Doctor in the sick room and my Lawyer in the court room. You are my Rose of Sharon, my Wheel in the middle of a wheel. You are my Captain, my Daddy, my Father, My Encourager. You are the Alpha and the Omega, the First and the Last. You are the beginning and the ending of all things. You are the A to Z. You are the Author and the Finisher of my Faith. You are my Sustainer, my

Comforter, my Master, my Friend, my Confidant, my All in all, and the Lover of my soul.

I'm taking time out to sit at your feet. I want to praise You, worship You, magnify You, exalt You and lift You up. I'm here to lift up Your holy and precious name. I came to honor You and glorify You because You alone are worthy of all honor and glory. I came because You alone are the worthy One to be worshipped. I'm here simply because I know that You inhabit the praises of Your people.

You said in Your word, let everything that has breath praise the Lord. Well Father, you have given me breath and I'm going to praise you from the rising of the sun until the going down of the same sun. love You Dear Lord. All I want to do is please You. All I want to do is live for You. I adore You and I extol You, because You are Majesty. I acknowledge that I can't do anything without You. acknowledge that I am weak without You. I acknowledge that I am nothing without You.

You called me, You chose me, You equipped me to be an Ambassador of Your Kingdom. You gave me the power to tread upon serpents and scorpions. You gave me power through the Holy

Spirit to do Your work. Dear Lord, use me as You please. I am available to You.

I am sitting at Your feet with thanksgiving and praise in my heart to love You and let You know how much I appreciate You. I have words of praise and adoration on my lips for You. It is a great privilege to be Your servant and I just want to say thank you for all that You have done for me. I just want to say hallelujah! I just want to thank You for being God all by Yourself. Thank You Father for protection, correction, instruction and direction. Thank You for spiritual wisdom, knowledge and understanding. Thank You for a mind to keep on keeping on in Jesus name. Thank You for renewing my strength. Thank You for forgiving me for the sins that I have committed against You in word, thought and deed. Thank You for forgiving me for those sins that I have committed knowingly and unknowingly. If I had 10,000 tongues it still would not be enough to say thank You. If You never do anything else for me I still thank You.

Father, show me my heart. Reveal those things to me that are not of You. I give You permission to clean me up, Lord. Allow me to take the beam out of my own eye so that I can see my faults and shortcomings. Give me a clean heart Oh God and renew a right spirit within me. I humbly submit myself to You. Purge me and take out everything that is not like You. Reveal everything to me that might hinder me from seeking Your face. Everything that might hinder me from hearing Your voice or speaking Your word. Teach me to speak blessings instead of curses and positives instead of negatives. Teach me how to be part of the solution instead of part of the problem. Remove anything that might prevent me from completing Your work and Your will.

Father, I have not always done everything in the manner that You would have me to, but Lord I am striving to do better. I am committing myself to do things according to Your word. Perform spiritual surgery on me Lord and cut out everything that prevents me from moving forward. Remove all unclean habits, all unclean words, all unclean deeds and all unclean thoughts. I want to be real and I want to be right.

My earnest desire is to be more like You. I want to be blameless and pure in Your sight. I want to be more like Jesus. I want to be the servant that You would have me to be. I want to fulfill the call that You have for me. Work in me, on me and through me. I move myself out of Your way so that you can have Your way in my life. I decrease so that You can increase in me. I am saying less of me and more of You. Please take away every bad habit, slothfulness, selfishness, lust, pride, fear, jealousy and envy. Take away bitterness, unforgiveness, gossip and backbiting and I will stay focused on You. Grow me up in You. Give me a spiritual cleansing through Your Holy Spirit from the crown of my head to the soles of my feet.

Father, I am seeking to study Your word more with diligence and sincerity. For Your word declares that we must study to show ourselves approved unto You, a workman that does not need to be ashamed rightly dividing the word of truth. Your word also declares in all our getting that we are to get understanding. This is our only way to be more like You.

Lord, I have a desire to please You in all that I do. I am a soldier in Your army. You have set me apart for Your pleasure. I will do what You want me to do, go where You want me to go and speak what You tell me to speak. I thank you for my being joint heirs with

Christ in Your kingdom. I know that my citizenship is in heaven. This world is not my home. I'm just passing through until your glorious and magnificent return.

All of my help comes from You Lord. All of my strength comes from You Lord. All of my hope is in You Lord. All of my resources comes from You. I would have no tomorrows if it were not for You. You hold all of my tomorrows in the palm of Your hand. It is not by my power or by my might but it is by Your Spirit. I know that I can do all things through You Lord because it is You who gives me strength. It is You who gives me power. It is You who gave this mighty anointing on my life. I praise You because of Your Holy Spirit I am free indeed.

Father, I hunger and thirst after you, like a deer that pants for the water when he's thirsty. My soul longs for You. I sit at Your feet because only You can quench this thirst and this appetite that I have for you. Only You can fill my cup with living water to overflowing. Only You can satisfy my every desire. I bless Your holy name now and forever. I sit at Your feet because You've been better to me then I've been to myself. You are the only One who could love me unconditionally. You are the only One who loves me in spite of my mistakes. Father, I am Your child and I thank You for the peace, love, joy, happiness, longsuffering, patience, meekness and kindness that I have through You. I sit at Your feet yearning to learn more about You and Your ways.

Father, right now in Your mighty and powerful name, in the name that is above every other name, I bind every hindering spirit in my life. I bind every trick and every work of the devil. I come against every principality, against rulers of darkness of this world and against spiritual wickedness in high places. I loose a spirit of discernment and tact. I know that my fight is not against flesh and blood, but against the wiles of evil. Father, I am aware that I must keep on my full armor so that I can withstand the attacks of the enemy. So that I can stand against demonic forces.

Thank You for teaching me how to gird my loins about with truth. Thank You for every piece of my spiritual armor. You have provided "spiritual gear" for spiritual protection. It is up to me to put it on to protect myself against the fiery darts of the adversary. Therefore, I have on my breastplate of righteousness. My feet are covered with the preparation of the gospel of peace. I have taken the shield of faith and have covered my head with the helmet of salvation. The sword of the Spirit is in my hand and I am ready for battle. I thank You Lord because I know that even though weapons may form they will not prosper because the battle is already won through you Dear Savior.

I believe that whatever You have for me it is for me. I believe that every door that You open no man can close it and every door that You close no man can ever open it again. Father, I come against all manner of sickness and disease that has tried to attack my body and take me out of this race. I bind up every attack on my mind. I bind every lie ever told against me. I come against the spirit of confusion, oppression, depression, suicide and poverty. I come against everything that is not of You and I resist it in Your name. I loose the fruit of the Spirit in my life. I lose wellness, soundness, and well being.

I believe that every stronghold is torn down by the Holy Spirit. speak deliverance to a dead situation and I loose it in the name of Jesus. I speak freedom into existence. I speak peace into existence.

speak blessings and prosperity over my life and the life of my family in Jesus' name.

Father, thank you for this time to be able to sit at Your feet. This time is a wonderful time, an intimate time, a time of refreshing and renewal. A time of restoration. I thank You Father that walls of bondage are tumbling down around me. The prison walls that have kept me captive is being torn down in Jesus' mighty name. I thank You for my being set free never to be in chains again. I thank You Lord for ruling and reigning in my life. I thank You for being the Captain of my soul. Thank You for being my Master and my Redeemer. Thank You for allowing me to be in Your presence. Thank You for allowing me to come into Your holy presence. Thank You for allowing me to empty myself out before You and for cleaning up my mess.

I thank You Lord for fully preparing me to do Your work. I thank You because now I can minister to others who are going through something and witness them be delivered and set free by the power of the Holy Spirit. I thank You for teaching me how to walk in the fullness of my calling. I thank You because now I see satan's kingdom being torn down in the spirit.

Father, I thank You for Your special loving touch during this time with You. I *will* go forth and walk in Your Spirit so that I will not fulfill the lusts of the flesh. I *will* go forth knowing that greater is He that is in me then He that is in the world. I *will* go forth knowing that perfect love casts out all fear. I *will* go forth knowing that all things work together for my good because I love You.

Father, thank You for my marching orders. Thank You for the great things that You have done while I sat in Your presence. Thank You for wiping every tear from my eyes and for reassuring me that I am Your child and I do belong to You. I will never forget all that You have done for me and all that You have brought me through. I will always give Your name the honor and the glory. Thank You Lord for my opportunity to sit at Your feet and bask in Your presence. Thank You for reminding me who You created me to be. Now I see a new beginning and I'm eagerly looking forward to what's to come. Now I can experience my happiness and I am set free in You.

Carmelia Bivins

"I AM SOMEBODY BECAUSE OF THE GREAT I AM!'

One thing have I desired of the Lord, that will I seek after; that I may dwell in the house of the Lord all the days of my life, to behold the beauty of the Lord, and to inquire in his temple. For in the time of trouble he shall hide me in his pavillion: in the secret of his tabernacle shall he hide me; he shall set me up upon a rock.

(Psalms 27:4,5)

ABOUT THE AUTHOR

"Now is Your Time, This Is Your Season!"

Minister Bivins is a powerfully anointed preach the uncompromising word of God. Minister Bivins servant and vessel called by God to teach and has been teaching and preaching the word of God for 10 years. Minister Bivins is an ordained and licensed minister. She is a dynamic evangelist, encourager and exhorter. Her special gifts are Intercessory Prayer, Healing and Deliverance.

She loves the Lord with all her heart and has dedicated her life to Him. Minister Bivins stands on the word of God that proclaims…*and we know that all things work together for good to those who love God, to those who are called according to His purpose. (Romans 8:28)*

Minister Bivins is a member of Nu-Way Christian Ministries in San Diego, California. She sits on the Ministerial staff and is under the anointed leadership of Pastor/Evangelist Steve O. Cooper.

The Lord has given her a vision for Higher HOPE Ministry. (Healed Of Past Entanglements). This ministry will be a safe house mainly geared towards the abused, displaced, hurting woman. It's goal is to provide and assist in every area from housing to job placement to furthering their education and counseling just to name a few of the many aspects of the program. The program will minister to the *total woman.*

Minister Bivins has two beautiful children Elizabeth and David. She currently attends International Theological Seminary headquartered in Bradenton, Florida. Where she is pursuing her Bachelor's of Theology Degree. Minister Bivins' ultimate goal is to one day become a Christian Clinical Counselor; serving the young & the old. Reaching & restoring the lost.

God has bestowed a gift upon her of writing by divine inspiration. "*Sitting At His Feet*", is one of her first books written with women in mind. She is currently working on her second book entitled:

"Elevating to God's Standards" (Reaching to Higher Heights and Deeper Depths in God's Kingdom).

Minister Bivins desires to be the woman of God that He is calling her to be—living totally by the word of God and winning the lost to Christ. Minister Bivins is available for speaking engagements or for ordering additional books by contacting: By e-mail PRAYEDUP2@cox.net. By mail: P. O. Box 250, El Cajon, Ca 92022

www.ingramcontent.com/pod-product-compliance
Lightning Source LLC
Chambersburg PA
CBHW051433280526
45785CB00003B/1267